STAND AGAINST

POLLUTION

AND

WASTE

Georgia Amson-Bradshaw

FRANKLIN WATTS

Franklin Watts

First published in Great Britain in 2020 by The Watts Publishing Group

Copyright © The Watts Publishing Group 2020

Produced for Franklin Watts by
White-Thomson Publishing Ltd
www.wtpub.co.uk

Editor: Georgia Amson-Bradshaw/Izzi Howell
Designer and illustrator: Mimi Butler

ISBN 978 1 4451 6823 4 (HB) and 978 1 4451 6824 1 (PB)

Printed in Dubai

Franklin Watts
An imprint of
Hachette Children's Group
Part of The Watts Publishing Group
Carmelite House
50 Victoria Embankment
London EC4Y 0DZ

An Hachette UK Company
www.hachette.co.uk
www.franklinwatts.co.uk

CONTENTS

KNOW YOUR TARGETS: Pollution and waste

Humans produce a lot of waste, and we're not just talking the stuff we throw in the bin. Waste chemicals and gases are constantly being pumped out in huge amounts around the world. When waste gets out into the environment, it becomes pollution, which hurts people and the planet.

WHAT A WASTE

Packaging, used or broken objects, uneaten food and all the things we throw away at home or at school are obvious kinds of waste. But what we don't see is that before the things we buy even get to us, a whole load more waste will have been produced while the objects were being manufactured.

THINK AND ACT

What was the last thing you threw away? Could you have **reused** it or **recycled** it instead?

MAKING THINGS

Take a single cotton T-shirt, for example. Growing cotton plants creates waste because some parts of the plant aren't used. Spinning and dyeing the fabric uses water and chemicals that become liquid waste. Making the fabric into a garment leaves waste fabric in the offcuts that aren't used. The T-shirt is wrapped in packaging to be transported and sold – which also becomes waste.

POLLUTION: THE MAIN CULPRITS

Air pollution is caused by harmful gases being released into the air, while water pollution is caused by chemicals or rubbish being dumped or leaked into waterways and the ocean. The dumping of litter or chemicals from farming and industry on the land and in the soil is land pollution.

Human beings create a lot of waste and pollution, which is bad for our health and the health of other animals and plants. Read on for ways to stand against pollution and waste.

WHERE DOES POLLUTION COME FROM?

Pollution is everywhere. Even in the Arctic, or in the middle of the ocean, the effects of human pollution can be found. So how does all this pollution get released into the environment?

VEHICLE EMISSIONS
One of the biggest sources of pollution is from vehicle engines. Vehicles burn fuels such as diesel and petrol, which release toxic gases, particulates (tiny bits of soot) and greenhouse gases (which cause climate change) into the air.

THERE ARE OVER A BILLION CARS ON THE ROAD WORLDWIDE.

INDUSTRIAL POLLUTION
The majority of our electricity is produced in power plants that burn fossil fuels such as gas, oil and coal. Like car engines, these create air pollution. Industry (that's factories such as chemical plants, metals and plastic factories, mills and mines) also releases polluting gases. Industry is a key source of water pollution, too, as chemicals from industrial processes leak or are dumped into waterways and the ocean.

AGRICULTURE

In many countries, agriculture is the largest source of water pollution. Pesticides applied to crops spread into the surrounding environment. Fertilisers, animal manure and eroded soil washes off farmland and into waterways, causing 'eutrophication'. This is when extra nutrients in water cause algae to grow too much, blocking out sunlight and using up all the oxygen in the water. This kills off water creatures such as fish and plants.

WASTE MANAGEMENT

Solid waste, or litter, is another type of pollution that ends up on the land and in the sea. Many places around the world don't have good waste management, and litter is often simply dumped on the land or in waterways, where it makes its way eventually to the ocean. Scientists estimate that up to 2.41 million tonnes of plastic waste enter the ocean each year from rivers.

THINK AND ACT

Do you see a lot of **litter** in your area? Could you pick some of it up and **put it in the bin**, instead of just leaving it where it is? Why not solve the problem yourself, rather than leaving it to someone else?

IMPACTS OF AIR POLLUTION

How serious can some gases in the air be? After all, there's so much air in the world! The answer: very serious. 4.6 million people die every year directly because of air pollution, and that's only the start.

HUMAN HEALTH

Have you ever found yourself coughing because of vehicle exhaust, or blown your nose, only to find your snot is all black? Yuck! That's air pollution. It can have very serious effects on our lungs, causing asthma, respiratory diseases such as emphysema, bronchitis and lung cancer.

As well as lung problems, it can increase the risk of heart attacks, strokes and diseases including Parkinson's and Alzheimer's. Air pollution is particularly risky for young children and babies in the womb, affecting brain development. Governments around the world monitor air pollution levels, and have targets to reduce it, because it is so important for improving citizens' health.

THINK ABOUT IT

HOW MANY OF YOUR FRIENDS AND CLASSMATES HAVE ASTHMA? DID YOU KNOW THAT THREE TIMES MORE PEOPLE HAVE ASTHMA TODAY THAN 50 YEARS AGO?

WILDLIFE

Plants and animals are at added risk from air pollution due to the effect of acid rain. When certain pollutants in the atmosphere mix with rain, it becomes acidic. When the rain falls on forests, lakes and streams, it can destroy trees, and make the water toxic to the fish and other creatures that live in it. Birds and animals that rely on the plants and the fish for food are also affected.

DAMAGE TO ATMOSPHERE

Ozone is a type of gas. High up in the Earth's atmosphere, there is a band containing ozone gas called the ozone layer. The way ozone reacts with sunlight protects the Earth below from the harshest UV rays.

However, when certain types of air pollution get into the atmosphere, they react with the ozone, causing the ozone layer to break down. This allows dangerous UV rays to get through, causing skin cancer and harming ecosystems. For example, extra UV rays can stop plankton from reproducing. Plankton make up the bottom rung of many food chains, so this reduces food for other animals all the way up the food chain.

>> Greenhouse gas emissions are one of the most serious types of air pollution, as they cause climate change. Read more about them on pages 38–41.

MEASURE AIR POLLUTION

Compare pollution in places you visit. You won't be able to measure gases but you can measure particulates (tiny pieces of solid pollution) such as dust and soot.

You'll need: white card, scissors, a hole punch, string, a permanent marker and Vaseline.

STEP 1

Cut the white card into twelve 6 cm x 6 cm squares. Punch a hole in the top of each one. Tie a piece of string through the hole, creating a loop so you can hang it off a tree branch or similar.

STEP 2

With an adult's help, think about four locations for your experiment (such as your bedroom, a friend's garden next to a busy road, your school's car park, and so on).

STEP 3

Use the marker to draw a small square on each piece of card. Smear a thin layer of Vaseline inside the square.

STEP 4

Hang three squares in each of your chosen locations, and leave them there for 7–10 days. (You might want to label them with **'science experiment – please do not touch'** on the back.)

STEP 5

Collect the squares after 10 days. Examine each card with the magnifying glass. You should find small particles stuck in the Vaseline. These are pieces of air pollution. **In which area did your card capture the most air pollution?**

Check **waqi.info** for real time information about air pollution around the world.

STAND AGAINST: AIR POLLUTION

Are you driven to school in a car, or do you walk, cycle or take a bus or train? In the past, it was much more common to walk or cycle to school compared to now. But with so many parents driving, there is more air pollution from cars around schools.

TOXIC AIR

The exhaust fumes from cars on the school run create areas of heavy pollution around schools, which exposes pupils to very high air pollution levels. This is especially dangerous for children, as air pollution affects their development. **So what can you do about it?**

 Why not encourage your schoolmates to walk to school by organising a **Walk to School Day?**

On a **Walk to School Day,** everyone walks (or cycles or takes public transport) to school. You can use the day to draw attention to the **health and environmental benefits of walking to school**.

STEP 1

Get your headteacher to approve the **Walk to School Day**. If they need some persuading, explain to them the health benefits for children and the benefits for the environment.

STEP 2

Promote the event to other students and parents. You could put up **posters** and **give out flyers**, or put an article in the school newsletter. It's good to talk about things that will motivate your schoolmates and their parents. Are they interested in health issues, or the environment? Is their local concern about road safety? Try to tap in to the issues that are important to your school community.

STEP 3

If you want, you could plan some 'walking buses' or 'park and strides'. **A walking bus** is where a group of children and a couple of adults meet at an agreed time and place, then walk to school in a group. It's safe and fun to do. **Park and stride** is good for people who live too far away from school to walk all the way. Instead, the parents can park a walkable distance away from school and the child walks the rest. It means that air pollution from the cars isn't all concentrated around the school.

STEP 4

Remind people the day before. **Hang up some banners** to greet everyone when they arrive at school the next day.

IMPACTS OF WATER POLLUTION

Water is essential to all life on Earth. But water pollution is a growing threat to us and other living creatures.

DIRTY WATER

2.3 billion people around the world don't have access to proper toilets. Even in places with toilets and sewage systems, the waste water isn't always treated properly. When sewage and waste water get into the environment, it can spread diseases such as cholera, dysentery, typhoid and polio.

Dirty drinking water is estimated to cause 502,000 deaths each year.

UNDERGROUND POLLUTION

Groundwater (water that is found underground inside porous rocks) can be polluted by chemical and industrial spills, or often by runoff from cities and roads. Roads get covered in bits of tyre, spilled fuel and exhaust emissions. When it rains, this pollution is washed onto the land where it can seep down into groundwater.

DETERGENTS

When we clean our homes, do our laundry and wash our dishes, we don't usually think about what happens to the chemicals and detergents that we wash down the drain. When the detergents aren't treated properly in waste water plants, they can poison aquatic life such as frogs and fish.

FARM WASTE

Over a third of the world's land is used for agriculture, and the runoff of animal manure, fertilisers, pesticides and other chemicals can cause big problems. As well as causing eutrophication (see page 7), pesticides can escape into the environment and kill wildlife.

OIL SPILLS

A very obvious type of water pollution is the oil spills that we see every so often on the news. Very major oil spills are quite rare, but when they do happen, they have very serious effects. Animals that swallow the oil are poisoned. Oil also destroys the insulating ability of birds' feathers and the fur on animals such as sea otters. Without the ability to repel water and insulate from the cold water, birds and mammals die from hypothermia.

>> **Less than one per cent of oil-soaked birds survive, even after BEING CLEANED.**

INVESTIGATE WATER POLLUTION

How polluted is the water in your area? What is the quality of your drinking water? Try these activities to find out.

Whenever collecting samples from rivers and lakes, ALWAYS wear gloves, have an adult present and take care at the water's edge.

In this experiment, compare the quality of your tap water, some bottled water and water from a local stream or beach.

You'll need: Three jars, water from a local river or beach, bottled water, tap water and water testing strips (available online, such as the Watersafe brand).

STEP 1
Collect your water samples in jars to be tested. It is essential to have an adult present when collecting water from a river or beach. Be very careful around the water's edge.

STEP 2
Use a strip to test each water sample as per the strip packet instructions (usually the strip is dipped in the water for 60 seconds).

STEP 3
Compare the colours on the strips to the chart in the testing kit. The colour of the strip will show you the levels of contaminants such as lead, nitrates (which often come from fertilisers used in farming), as well as how acidic the water is.

INDICATOR SPECIES

Scientists use the presence of 'indicator species' to judge how polluted water is. This is because some animals can survive only in clean water, whereas others thrive in polluted water. See if you can find indicator species in a nearby stream or lake with this project.

You'll need: A white plastic tray with deep sides, rubber gloves, a digital camera and internet access.

STEP 1

With gloves on, collect some water in the tray – about 2 cm deep. Take care at the water's edge.

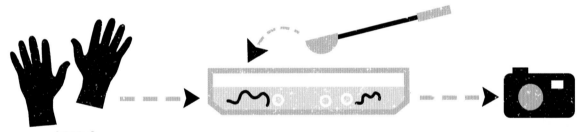

STEP 2

Take pictures of the creatures that you find, then count and release them. On a computer with internet access, see if you can identify the creatures. In particular, look for mayfly larvae and stonefly nymphs. These are indicators of clean water. If you find freshwater shrimp or caddis fly larvae, this indicates some pollution. If you find bloodworms or rat-tailed maggots, this indicates high pollution.

MAYFLY LARVA   FRESHWATER SHRIMP   RAT-TAILED MAGGOT

OCEAN PLASTIC POLLUTION

You may have heard about the problem with plastic pollution in the ocean. But although people are waking up to the problem, we are still using millions of tonnes of plastic every year, with huge amounts of it going into the ocean.

PLASTIC EVERYWHERE

We use plastic to make everything, from clothes, packaging and toys to vehicles such as planes and cars! Its versatility and durability means it's very useful. But even though plastic takes hundreds of years to break down, we treat it like it's disposable, making plastic items and throwing them away after one use.

ESCAPED WASTE

In less economically developed countries (LEDCs), the lack of waste management systems means a lot of waste simply gets dumped on the land or in rivers, then washes into the ocean. Even in countries with better rubbish collection, plastic still escapes into the environment through littering and being washed down the drain.

THINK AND ACT

Do you ever see people at school throwing plastic bottles and other containers in the bin? Ask them to **recycle them instead.**

PROBLEM FOR WILDLIFE

Up to 12.7 million tonnes of plastic end up in the ocean each year. Much of this is litter from the land, but a huge amount is also lost or dumped fishing gear. Plastic fishing nets go on catching fish even when they have been dumped, killing thousands of animals every year.

STARVING SEAGULLS

To many animals, such as turtles and seabirds, plastic looks like food. Other creatures that filter feed, such as whales, can't help but swallow plastic while they are eating. The plastic these animals swallow can't be digested, eventually filling up their stomachs and starving them to death.

TOXIC SNACKS

It isn't just the big bits of plastic that we can see that are a problem. Tiny fragments of plastic called microplastics absorb toxic chemicals, and are then eaten by small creatures such as shellfish and plankton. When the small creatures are eaten by bigger fish and birds, the toxic microplastics are passed up the food chain – eventually to us! The chemicals in these microplastics can have harmful health effects for the animals that accidentally eat them.

>> **If nothing changes, by 2050 there will be more plastic in the ocean by weight than fish.**

Solving the problem of water pollution might seem like a huge problem, but there are lots of things we can all individually do to help. And the more people take action against pollution, the more others will be encouraged to change their behaviour, too.

CHOOSE ECO-FRIENDLY DETERGENTS

There are a wide range of eco-friendly cleaning products available, including dish soaps, laundry liquids and surface cleaners. They still clean effectively, but if they escape into the environment they won't harm wildlife. Ask your family to buy eco-friendly cleaning products when they next go shopping.

AVOID PLASTICS

Explain to your parents the problem of plastic pollution, and try to avoid using so much plastic as a family. Could your family buy loose fruit and veg, instead of stuff wrapped in plastic? Avoid buying single drinks in plastic bottles such as fruit juices and fizzy drinks, and carry a reusable bottle filled with cordial instead. Ask your parents not to buy individually-wrapped snacks for your lunch – why don't you make your own snacks to take instead?

ORGANISE A BEACH CLEAN

Take action against the rubbish that has already escaped into the environment by organising a beach clean. If you don't live near a beach, you could do a river clean instead. Here's how to organise a clean up.

➤➤ **FOR ACTIVITIES NEAR THE WATER, ALWAYS have an adult present and take care at the water's edge.**

You'll need: rubbish bags, gloves, litter pickers (optional)

STEP 1

Pick a time and date. Nice weather will make more people want to come. Low tide is the best time for a beach clean, as that is when more rubbish is exposed on the beach.

STEP 2

Spread the word. Get as many people to come as you can by promoting it at school, on social media and on local websites, with the help of an adult. If you anticipate a lot of people coming, it's a good idea to let the local council or landowner know you're doing it.

STEP 3

Get your supplies: make sure there are enough gloves and bags for everyone. It might be nice to provide snacks, too.

STEP 4

Make it fun! Turn it into a game by awarding prizes to whoever collects the most, or whoever finds a list of particular items (such as plastic bottles, straws, etc.) first.

THROWAWAY CULTURE

What do you do with things you have broken, but don't want anymore? At best, you probably give them to a charity shop, but it's just as likely you throw them in the bin. But this habit of always getting new stuff and then throwing it away is a problem.

TAKE, MAKE, DISPOSE

Remember the problem of 'disposable' plastic, that we use then throw away? We have the same basic problem with everything we use. All our stuff follows a 'linear system': the materials to make it are extracted from the land, are made into things, transported and sold, used and then thrown away. But the big problem is that there won't always be more resources to extract, and the 'away' we throw things to just means landfill: big rubbish dumps that take up space, and pollute the local air and water supply.

DAMAGED PLANET

Making items uses a lot of raw materials, such as oil and minerals from underground, or wood from forests. Extracting these materials requires energy and land, and causes pollution. Turning the materials into objects and then transporting them uses even more energy. Worldwide, most energy is generated by burning fossil fuels, which releases greenhouse gases. These stay in the Earth's atmosphere, trapping heat from the Sun and causing climate change. Read more about this on pages 38–41.

TOO MUCH STUFF

Not only do we waste resources by constantly making new stuff then throwing it away, the sheer amount of stuff we consume means we are using natural resources, such as wood from forests, far faster than the Earth can replace them. Globally, we are using 1.7 times more resources each year than the planet can sustain. This is called 'overconsumption'.

THINK AND ACT

Do you have any unwanted clothes and toys? **How could you make sure they don't get wasted?**

WHAT DO WE WASTE?

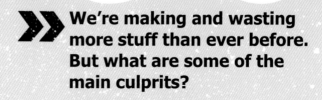 **We're making and wasting more stuff than ever before. But what are some of the main culprits?**

FAST FASHION

The world now consumes **80 billion items of clothing every year**. That's four times as many as just twenty years ago. A lot of this increase is driven by 'fast fashion', where shops sell very cheap versions of the latest trends, which people wear only a few times and then throw away. Very little textile waste is recycled either – about 12 per cent around the world. Most of it is sent to landfill.

PACKAGING

A huge amount of what we throw away is packaging, particularly food packaging. Plastic wrappers keep our food fresh, but only 10 per cent of plastic is recycled globally. Most gets sent to landfill, where it can take hundreds of years to break down, if it ever breaks down at all.

THINK ABOUT IT

It takes an average of 10,000 litres of water to make 1 kg of cotton. The cotton industry also accounts for 25 per cent of the world's insecticide use: toxic chemicals for killing pests, which damage the environment.

ELECTRONICS

Unwanted electronic goods, or e-waste, is one of the fastest growing types of waste product. Only 20 per cent of this type of waste is recycled, but making electrical devices has a big environmental impact.

Rare metals used in smartphones are often mined using very toxic chemicals, and are taken from natural places such as the Amazon rainforest. Vast amounts of energy are needed to extract the materials, contributing to climate change.

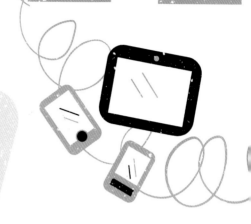

THINK AND ACT

If you are thinking about replacing an electrical device such as a mobile phone, think about whether you could **repair or improve it, rather than get an entirely new one.**

BUILDING WASTE

The construction industry (that's building houses and roads) produces a lot of waste in the form of rubble from the building site, unused materials and chemicals used in the construction process. Concrete particularly is a problem. It is the most used material in the world after water, but old concrete is rarely recycled.

MEASURE YOUR WASTE

How much waste does your family produce each week? You'll probably be surprised. Try this project to find out how much waste you are generating, and look for ways you could reduce it.

 You'll need: Separate boxes or bags to separate different types of waste and a set of weighing scales.

 STEP 1 Explain to your family the problem of waste, and how you'd like to measure your combined output over a week. As an option, you could ask them to bring rubbish they produce at work or school home too, so it can be included in the weigh-in.

 STEP 2 Set out some bags or boxes for everyone to put the waste in. It's a good idea to separate the waste into categories, such as recyclables (glass, cardboard, tins, and so on), non-recyclables/things that are rarely recycled (plastic films, Styrofoam, coffee cups, straws) and food waste. Include everything that gets thrown out that week, even big items such as furniture.

Wash any dirty containers before putting them in the bins so they don't smell while you collect them.

 STEP 3 At the end of the week, weigh each of the different containers. Which type of rubbish did you produce the most of? You could even take a family selfie surrounded by the rubbish to share on social media, encouraging others to do the same!

STEP 4 As a family, go through the items you have collected. Seeing all the rubbish in front of them might make them more aware of how much waste they produce. Discuss how you might be able to cut your waste down as a family – there are some ideas for how to do this on the next page!

If you feel inspired by trying this at home, how about trying to get your whole class doing it as a joint project, too?

STAND AGAINST: WASTE

Cutting down the amount of waste we produce depends on two things: buying less stuff in the first place, and being careful about what we do with the stuff we already have.

If you need something, think through it like this. **Start at the bottom of the pyramid, and work up.**

BUY SECOND-HAND

If you do have to buy something, you can probably get it **second-hand**. This saves a lot of money and resources too. Only buy new as a last resort.

SWAP. RENT. BORROW

If you really need something that you don't already have (perhaps you need some special kit for a school trip), could you **borrow** it from someone, or **rent** it instead? Borrowing and renting is much more eco-friendly, and saves your house getting full of unused clutter, too.

REUSE WHAT YOU HAVE

Do you **REALLY** need a new pair of trainers, or do you just want those new ones because they're cool? Everyone likes to have the newest, trendiest stuff, but the less you care about having the best, shiniest, newest things all the time, the **happier** you'll be, honest!

When you are thinking of getting rid of something, think through it like this. Again, **start at the bottom as the best and most efficient choice**, and work your way up.

DISPOSAL

Throwing stuff away is the absolute **last resort**. Some people manage to produce almost no un-recyclable waste at all. How little can you make?

RECYCLE

Once you can't reuse an item anymore, send it for **recycling**. Recycling still uses energy and resources though, so it's less efficient than reusing things.

REUSE

If you've bought a drink in a plastic bottle, for example, don't throw the bottle out. **Refill** it at home and use it as a drinks bottle. Wherever you can, try to **reuse** the things you **already own**.

REFUSE

Try not to accumulate wasteful things in the first place. If someone offers you a plastic bag or straw you don't need, **refuse it**.

A DIFFERENT SYSTEM

At the moment, it's really difficult to live a zero-waste lifestyle, because unfortunately, the world today just isn't set up for it. But it doesn't have to be this way.

MAKE

CIRCULAR ECONOMY

Remember that linear system we learned about on page 22 – 'take, make and dispose'?

Imagine if instead of chucking away all the old objects and packaging we buy, we sent them back to the companies to be **reused and refurbished**? Or perhaps sent them to an entirely different company who could make use of the old packaging or pieces in a new way?

This idea is called a '**circular economy**', because the resources in it go round and round between maker and consumer (that's you, the buyer), instead of ending up in landfill.

USE

RECOVER

DEPOSIT SYSTEMS

Bottle deposit schemes for drinks bottles and cans exist in some countries, where people pay a little bit extra for the bottle, and get the money back when they return it. In Norway, successful deposit schemes mean that 97 per cent of all drinks bottles and cans are returned and reused or recycled.

THINK AND ACT

Milk deliveries in **returnable** glass bottles are getting more popular again, after a decline in their use. Look online to see if there is one in your area, and if so, **ask your parents if you could sign up to it.**

A BIGGER SCALE

In order for things like deposit schemes to really make a difference to how much waste we produce, they need to be easy and widespread. For example, the scheme in Norway is successful because there are machines and counters for people to return bottles in supermarkets and other accessible locations. Companies who sell drinks in bottles pay less tax when more bottles are returned, so they make it easy for the customers.

Governments and businesses can both help make the necessary changes to reduce our huge waste output — and it's up to us to tell politicians and companies that it's what we want.

WHY IS FOOD WASTED?

>> **Did you know that up to a third of all the food produced in the world gets wasted? This is despite the fact that globally, one billion people don't get enough to eat. So why does this happen?**

AT THE FARM

In more economically developed countries (MEDCs), food gets wasted before it even reaches the supermarkets. In order to ensure that they can supply however much the supermarkets want, farmers grow lots of food. But the supermarkets' orders are often unpredictable, and the farmers often grow more food than they can sell. They can't make any money from the unwanted food, so it doesn't get picked and sold.

In LEDCs, the facilities for storing and transporting produce isn't always good enough, so sometimes food goes off before it is sold.

IN THE FACTORY

Not all food is sold in the same state it came off the plant. It might be trimmed, chopped, or used in a ready meal or a tin of soup. Wastage happens in the food processing plants and factories, too, as edible trimmings are thrown away, or when the machines processing the food into new dishes don't work properly.

AT THE SHOP

When you go to the supermarket, you don't expect to see empty shelves, or a very limited range of products. But to keep shelves heaving with a large variety of things means it's very likely that some of those items will reach their 'sell-by' date before they get sold. Some supermarkets will donate expired food to charities, but often it just goes into the bin.

AT HOME

A lot of food waste happens at home, too. When people are tempted to 'buy one get one free' at the supermarket, they sometimes end up buying more than they need, and throwing it out because they can't eat it before it goes off.

When we cook more than we can eat, it's often put in the bin, instead of being saved for leftovers, especially in MEDCs where people can afford to waste food. In the USA, for example, 55 million tonnes of food is thrown away each year!

THINK AND ACT

Do you or your parents often put more food on your plate than you can actually eat? **Start with smaller portions:** it's better to go for seconds than to throw food in the bin.

IMPACTS OF FOOD WASTE

The fact that food is unfairly shared around the world means that many go hungry, while others eat too much and suffer from obesity and related illnesses. But food waste is linked to even more problems.

OVERFISHING

Of the fish that we take out of the sea to eat, 35 per cent are wasted. This is very bad news, considering a third of the world's fish stocks are being overfished, meaning they are being taken out of the ocean faster than the population can recover. If we continue fishing and wasting fish catches at the same rate, we will drive all the world's fish stocks to extinction by 2048.

EXTINCTION

One third of the world's land is used for agriculture, and this figure keeps growing. In order to make room to grow more crops, animal habitats are being destroyed. Scientists estimate that around the world, 150–200 wildlife species are going extinct every day, in large part caused by the effects of farming. By producing more food than we need, we are unnecessarily driving more species to extinction.

ERODING SOIL

Soil stores carbon in the form of broken-down plant material, which stops it getting into the atmosphere as a greenhouse gas (read more about this on page 38). Soil is also necessary to grow crops and to absorb rainwater, which prevents flooding. But common farming techniques wear the soil away, releasing carbon dioxide and making it harder to grow food. By overproducing from stressed soils now, we will make it hard to feed everyone in the future.

THINK AND ACT

The world's population is set to rise to nearly **10 BILLION by 2050**. We can feed that many people, but only if we change the way we produce and share food. **Tell people what you have learned about food waste** to encourage them to change their behaviour, too.

WATER WASTE

Agriculture accounts for about 70 per cent of fresh water use around the world. In many places, water from lakes or underground water stores is being used up faster than it is replaced, putting millions of people's water supply at risk. Because food uses so much water to produce, wasted food equals even more wasted water. For example, one kilo of wasted beef also wastes the 50,000 litres of water it took to produce.

STAND AGAINST: FOOD WASTE

It isn't that difficult to reduce food waste at home, it's just a matter of changing habits a little bit. Talk to your family about making some of the following changes.

Some ways to cut your waste

TIP ONE

Plan your meals. Check what food you already have in the cupboard, then **write a shopping list** for the exact things you need to make those meals. Why not get the whole family involved in this, with everyone suggesting a dinner that they can cook? Then, when shopping, only buy the items on the list. Having a plan like this will help stop impulse purchases that don't get used.

TIP TWO

Don't pile your plates really high when serving food. In fact, if you can **use smaller plates** that's even better. This will stop you serving yourself more than you can eat in one go. You can always have seconds if you are still hungry!

TIP THREE

Store leftovers and eat them for lunch or dinner the next day. Extra food that has been made at dinnertime makes a time-saving packed lunch, if stored properly in a sealed box. Just make sure to actually **eat the leftovers**.

Monday → Tuesday

TIP FOUR

Only use sell-by or **expiration dates** as guidelines. They are to do with food quality, not food safety, so just because a piece of food 'went off' a day or two ago, try smelling and tasting it before getting rid of it. If it smells and tastes fine, it should be fine to eat. More caution is advised around meat and dairy than other types of food.

TIP FIVE

If you have an outside space, **try composting** food peelings and other fruit and vegetable scraps. The compost can be used later to grow flowers or more food!

>> If you want to help fight food waste at a larger scale, why not look online to see if any food waste charities are active in your area? Some groups run activities such as 'gleaning', where excess fruit and veg that farmers can't sell to supermarkets are picked by volunteers and given to people in need.

POLLUTION, WASTE AND CLIMATE CHANGE

On Earth, all our natural systems are connected, so when we damage one part, it has knock-on effects. Because of this, the dirty truth is that pollution and waste contribute to a really big problem: climate change.

WHAT IS CLIMATE CHANGE?

One of the most serious types of man-made pollution are greenhouse gases that cause climate change. When we burn fossil fuels to power our vehicles or to drive electricity generators, they release carbon dioxide (CO_2) into the air. The Earth's atmosphere naturally has some CO_2 in it, but since the eighteenth century, we have been adding more and more.

CO_2 and other gases in the atmosphere are called 'greenhouse gases'. This is because they act almost like the glass of a greenhouse, letting heat in and trapping it close to the Earth. This is causing the Earth to slowly heat up, causing extreme weather and other devastating consequences around the globe.

THINK ABOUT IT

On average, around 1200 tonnes of CO_2 are released into the air every single second. That's the same weight as roughly 300 elephants.

METHANE, BLACK CARBON AND OZONE

CO_2 isn't the only type of greenhouse gas. Methane is 30 times more powerful than CO_2 as a greenhouse gas, and other gases such as black carbon (in soot) and ground-level ozone act as pollutants, which damage human health, and as heat-trapping gases in the atmosphere that drive storms, flooding and drought. Read more about this on the next page.

DANGEROUS WASTE

Remember how wasting resources and food leads to unnecessary greenhouse gas emissions? Well, waste's contribution to climate change doesn't stop there. When we send rubbish to landfill, it all gets piled up in a big hole in the ground. There isn't any oxygen in landfill, so the waste breaks down 'anaerobically', meaning without oxygen. This produces methane. Along with the burps and farts from livestock, this is one of the biggest sources of methane around the world.

THINK AND ACT

Because so much methane comes from livestock, you can reduce the amount you are responsible for by **eating less meat and dairy**.

IMPACTS OF GREENHOUSE GASES

Greenhouse gases are causing our atmosphere to heat up. Hot air can hold more water vapour than cold air before it reaches the point where it starts to rain. This means weather patterns around the world are changing, with some places experiencing droughts, and other places experiencing serious floods.

CROP FAILURE

The food that we grow depends on having the right kind of weather: a good amount of rain at the right time to water the plants, and the correct amount of sunshine to help them grow. But changing weather patterns mean some plants are not getting enough water, or are getting too much water and are being flooded. Crop failures lead to food shortages, and people going hungry.

THINK ABOUT IT
If humans are struggling to grow food in places where the weather is changing, how do you think the wild plants and animals are being affected?

OUT OF TIME

Many of the Earth's creatures and ecosystems are very sensitive to temperature. For example, some bird species hatch chicks at a certain time of year when there are the right number of hours of daylight. But the caterpillars that the chicks eat emerge when the temperature is right. Because the Earth is warmer, this is happening earlier in the springtime, and by the time the chicks have hatched, the caterpillars are all gone, leaving them without food. This in turn has an impact on other creatures further up the food chain.

WILD WEATHER

As weather becomes more unpredictable, it also becomes more extreme. Hotter air temperatures make hurricanes stronger, while drier conditions help wildfires to spread. Around the world, extreme weather events are becoming more common, causing more damage and death through droughts, heat waves, flooding and fire.

We all need to make changes in order to combat climate change. Here are some ways that you and your family can reduce your carbon footprint.

Some ways to cut your footprint

TIP ONE

Walk or cycle wherever possible, instead of getting a lift in a car. Public transport such as buses and trains also release fewer greenhouse gases per passenger than private vehicles.

TIP TWO

Get your family to wash the laundry in cool water, and dry it on an airer or line instead of in a tumble dryer. This will cut a lot of electricity usage.

TIP THREE

If your family fly a lot for holidays, ask your parents if you could do an overland trip by train or coach instead. The emissions from aeroplanes are particularly harmful because they are released high up in the sky, where they cause a more powerful warming effect.

TIP FOUR

Grow some of your own food. Gardening is a fun and rewarding hobby, as nothing tastes better than a sweet strawberry or juicy tomato that you have grown yourself! If you don't have anywhere to grow fruit and veggies, ask your parents to buy local, organic foods where possible. This means the food won't have travelled a long distance or been grown with wildlife-harming chemicals.

TIP FIVE

Ask for 'non-stuff' presents at Christmas and birthdays. This could be something like a day at a theme park or a zoo-keeping experience. Most experiences have a smaller carbon footprint than 'stuff' such as toys, clothes and games consoles, and even better, they don't end up as waste once they are broken or you don't want them any more.

»» One of the most important things you can do is talk to other people about climate change and your efforts to reduce your impact. The more people see others taking action, the more normal it becomes, and the more likely they are to take action themselves.

BE THE CHANGE, SPREAD THE WORD

>> **Campaigning for change and sharing solutions are just as important as taking action yourself. Here are some ways you can amplify your efforts.**

ZERO WASTE WEEK

Launched in 2008, Zero Waste Week is an annual event that happens around the world in September. People, community groups and businesses all try to produce zero waste (or as little waste as possible) over the week. Why not try it yourself? You could get your family to share your attempts online over the course of the week to inspire others to have a go themselves. Search for Zero Waste Week online for tips.

WRITE TO YOUR LOCAL POLITICIANS

Find out who your MP and local councillors are, and write to them. Politicians will only take action on pollution and waste if they think enough people care about it. Explain the problems that pollution and waste cause, and ask them to do something about it.

STREET THEATRE

This can be a really fun way to spread the message to people in your town or local area. Get a group of friends together, and write a short script for a play that explains the problems of pollution and waste. You could have people acting as polluters, as well as people acting as the people and animals that are affected by pollution.

Perform your play somewhere in the town centre. It's a good idea to have some printed materials with the key facts for interested passers-by to read, too. In many places you can do street theatre without asking permission, but it's good to check the rules in your local area first. Always have adults accompanying you.

HOST A SCREENING

Organise a film night at home or at school showing a film about the problems of pollution, waste and climate change. You could show a documentary, such as *Arctic Tale*, or even a fictional film with a relevant message, such as *WALL-E.* After the film, have everyone talk about how the film made them think and feel.

THINK AND ACT

Can you come up with some other creative ways to **spread the word about pollution and waste?**

Glossary

agriculture the practice of preparing the soil and growing crops or raising animals for food

asthma a condition that affects the airways (the tubes carrying air in and out of the lungs)

carbon footprint the amount of greenhouse gas emissions (particularly carbon dioxide) that each person is responsible for through their lifestyle

climate change the changes in weather patterns and temperatures around the world, caused by human activity

composting a process that turns food scraps into rich, new soil

contaminant a substance that pollutes something, making it impure

durability the ability to withstand heavy use without wearing away

emissions something that has been released or put out into the world, such as gases coming out of a car exhaust

eutrophication when extra nutrients get into water and cause too much growth in water plants

extinct when a type of living thing has completely died out

fertiliser a substance used to help plants grow bigger or stronger

fossil fuel a fuel such as oil or coal that was formed over millions of years from the remains of plants and animals

gleaning volunteer harvesting of food that would otherwise be wasted

greenhouse gas gases that, when in the atmosphere, trap the Sun's heat

insecticide a chemical used to kill insects

manufacture to make something

microplastics a tiny bit of plastic

overfishing taking fish out of the water faster than the species can replace itself through reproduction

ozone a gas made of oxygen atoms

ozone layer a layer of ozone gas high in the Earth's atmosphere which helps protect us from the Sun's strong rays

particulates very small bits of solid pollution such as dust or soot

pesticide a chemical used to kill unwanted creatures

plankton tiny plants and animals that live in water

refurbish to repair or upgrade existing objects so they can be used again

respiratory disease a disease that affects the lungs and airways

runoff water or other substances that drain off the land and into streams or groundwater

sewage waste water that is carried away from houses and cities in pipes

versatility the ability to be used in lots of ways

Further Information

BOOKS

This Book is Not Rubbish
Isabel Thomas (Wren & Rook, 2018)
Covering issues like plastics, pollution, global warming and endangered animals, this book is full of top tips for ditching plastic and reducing your rubbish.

EcoGraphics: Pollution
Izzi Howell (Franklin Watts, 2019)
Pollution is fast invading every part of the Earth, from the deepest ocean to the most remote desert to the very air we breathe. Can we reverse the damage before it's too late?

WEBSITES

trjfp.com
A project that started in Leeds, UK, the Real Junk Food Project is now a global network of volunteer-run 'Pay as you feel' cafés and food distribution centres, which take food that would otherwise be wasted and cook and distribute it. The food comes from gleaned fruit and veg, or supermarket stock that isn't sold before expiration. Visitors to the cafés and centres can pay whatever they can afford, thereby providing meals to people in need. Check the website to find a café or project near you.

feedbackglobal.org/campaigns/gleaning-network
Food waste organisation Feedback runs several campaigns, including its nationwide Gleaning Network. This gives volunteers all over the UK the opportunity to rescue fresh produce from farms and get it to good causes. Visit the website to find out about gleaning activities near you.

Note to parents and teachers: every effort has been made by the Publishers to ensure websites are suitable for children, that they are of the highest educational value, and that they contain no inappropriate or offensive material. However, because of the nature of the Internet, it is impossible to guarantee that the contents of these sites will not be altered. We strongly advise that Internet access is supervised by a responsible adult.

Index